HARPER COUNTS HER BLESSINGS

Written by Kristi Guillory Reid
Art by Jerry Craft

MAMA'S BOYZ, INC • NORWALK

HARPER COUNTS HER BLESSINGS

Written by Kristi Guillory Reid
Illustrated and designed by Jerry Craft
Edited by Ernestine Eisenhauer
Title design by Danni Ai

Summary: At the end of a seemingly ordinary day, four-year-old Harper doesn't think that she has much to be thankful for. Fortunately, her loving parents are there to point out all the wonderful things that happen each day that she should cherish. *Harper Counts Her Blessings* shows children the importance of taking the time each day as a family to reflect upon their blessings and to thank God.

ISBN-13: 978-1-7323184-2-7

First Edition
Printed in the United States

Published by Mama's Boyz, Inc
www.jerrycraft.com

Counting My Blessings

Thank you to God for putting the dream of writing in my heart. It started out as a whisper and grew to a roar that I could no longer ignore. Thank you for giving me the talent and drive to accomplish my goals.

Thank you to my Mother, Eva, for her constant prayers and spiritual guidance. Your love of the Lord has been a shining example to me throughout my life, and serves as a constant example to me as I raise my daughter.

Thank you to my Husband, Efrem, for supporting me with candor, humor, and love. Thank you for being my proofreader, copy editor, and most of all, a wonderful husband and father.

Thank you to my Father, Jesse, for always instilling in me to be the best and for giving me the gift of gab. I miss you every day.

Thank you to my Daughter, Harper, for changing my life and for allowing me to see the world anew through your beautiful, inquisitive eyes. You are my muse and I hope that I make you proud!

I hope that this book inspires you to make prayer and to give thanks a family activity. Taking time each day to reflect upon your blessings, and thanking God for them will help children to learn to appreciate what is truly important in life.

"I'm ready for bed now.
Can you read me a story?"

"You're not ready for bed yet, Harper.
You forgot to say your prayers."

"Oh, right, I know what to do."

'Watch!"

"First--
I get on
my knees."

"Then, I close
my eyes."

"Next, I get quiet so I can talk to God."

"Now, I'm ready!"

"But, Daddy, I don't know what to say."

"Sure you do. Just think of everything you did today that you're thankful for."

"You mean, like this?"
"Dear God, thank you for my big-girl bed. Now I can get up by myself *EVERY* day."

"And I like when Daddy makes his yummy pancakes. But I don't like syrup."

"I can make my own breakfast, too.
Even though sometimes
I miss the bowl."

"And thank you, Lord, for all the pretty things that Mommy puts in my hair."

"Oh, and dress-up day at school was so much fun.

I wore my superhero costume. Mommy and Daddy tell me that I can do and be anything.

I *KNOW* I can!"

"Dear Lord, I can write my name now.
Even if sometimes my *p's* still look like *q's*."

"Thank you for not letting Alexis get hurt when she fell down on the playground. I told her it was only a little boo-boo, so she stopped crying."

"I *LOVE* going to Grammie's house after school.
She lets me have cookies.
But, I have to practice my letters and numbers first."

"I'm so glad that I didn't get in trouble when she caught me playing dress-up in her closet."

"But I really like *MOMMY'S* shoes, too."

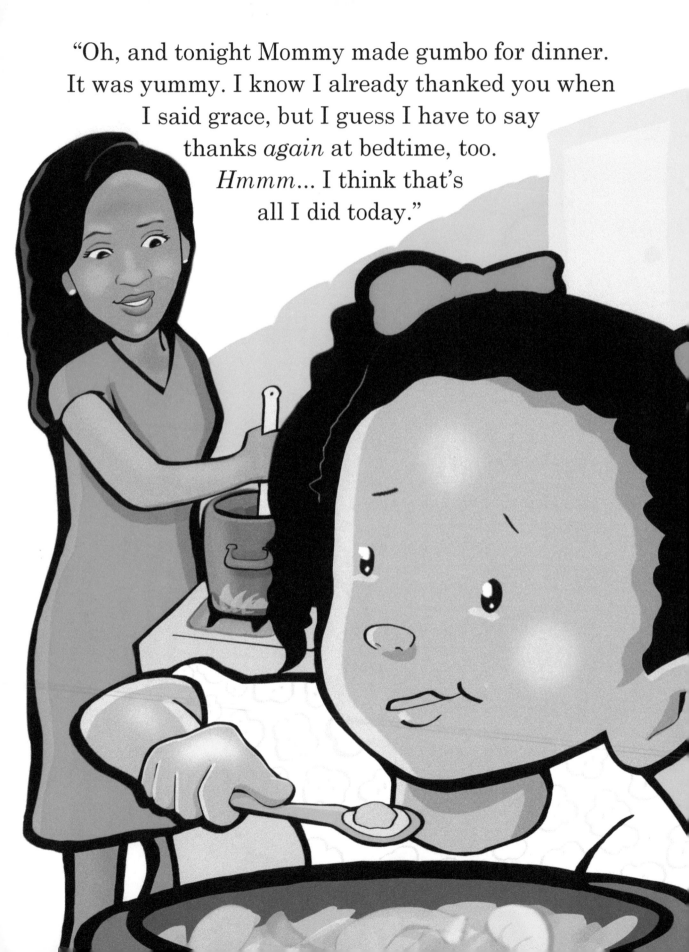

"Oh, and tonight Mommy made gumbo for dinner.
It was yummy. I know I already thanked you when
I said grace, but I guess I have to say
thanks *again* at bedtime, too.
Hmmm... I think that's
all I did today."

"Oops! And dear Lord, thank you for Mommy and Daddy. They are the best parents in the whole world. I love them *SO* much."

"And haven't you forgotten someone, Harper?"

"Yes! Thank you for my Princess doll, Mommy. She's my favorite because she looks just like me."

"No, sweetheart, we mean *YOU*."

"Me? Okay, Daddy! Lord, please bless me, too. Help me to grow big and strong and be a good girl."

KRISTI GUILLORY REID

AUTHOR: Kristi Guillory Reid has always loved to write and can now add the title "author" to her resume with her first book, *Harper Counts Her Blessings*. An accomplished attorney and public policy strategist, Kristi has experience in public, private and nonprofit healthcare organizations. Over the years, Kristi's work has appeared in a number of publications, including CNN.COM, The Washington Informer and Washington Parent.

When she noticed a lack of children's books that captured the spirit of black families, she used her love of writing, along with her experiences raising a toddler, to write her very first book. *Harper Counts Her Blessings* shows how the events of an ordinary day turn out not to be so ordinary when you truly reflect upon the blessings in your life. A proud native of Louisiana, Kristi resides in Northern Virginia with her husband, Efrem, and daughter, Harper.

For more information, you can find her on Instagram @kristigreid or email her at kristi.guillory.reid@gmail.com.

JERRY CRAFT

Photo by Hollis King

ARTIST: Jerry Craft has illustrated and/or written close to three dozen children's books, graphic novels and middle grade novels including his acclaimed anti-bullying book, "The Offenders: Saving the World While Serving Detention!" In 2014, Jerry illustrated "The Zero Degree Zombie Zone," for Scholastic which earned him recognition from the Junior Library Guild. He is the creator of Mama's Boyz, an award-winning comic strip that was distributed by King Features Syndicate from 1995 - 2013.

Jerry has won five African American Literary Awards and is also a co-founder and co-producer of the Schomburg's Annual Black Comic Book Festival which has drawn close to 40,000 fans since its inception in 2013. February 2019 will mark the release of "New Kid," a middle grade graphic novel the he wrote and illustrated for HarperCollins.

For more info visit: www.jerrycraft.com.

CPSIA information can be obtained
at www.ICGtesting.com
Printed in the USA
LVHW071448130323
741518LV00008B/175

9 781732 318427